A Journey Towards Unity and Reconciliation

BE Reconciled is a seven-conversation journey of processing unity and reconciliation in the Kingdom of God. The model teaches Bible-believing Christians how to "sit at the dinner table" to discuss complex issues by using biblical case studies. The BE Reconciled process activates, cultivates, and empowers individuals and teams in working out the journey towards unity and reconciliation.

Visit our website: http://www.bereconciledlexington.com

BE Reconciled
A Journey Towards Unity and Reconciliation
The Process Guide

Copyright © 2021 by Dr. Conrad and Kandace Davies.

Acknowledgments & Thanksgiving

Dr. Conrad Davies:

I want to offer thanks to many of our dear friends who helped us edit, revise, rethink, and reconsider our perspectives. We had hours of conversations with you, so we sincerely thank you for loving and supporting us in this endeavor. May the Lord bless you, Friends (you know who you are).

I am most thankful to my wife, Kandace, for partnering with me in all that we do. It is such a joy doing this work with you. I am a blessed man because of you.

Lastly, I thank You, Lord, for putting this work on our hearts. You said for me to give You something to work with, so here it is. I ask that You do with this work what You desire. Please impact our friends' hearts by the power of Your Word. May You be glorified through this endeavor. I bless You, Lord, for Your desire to see lives changed is greater than I could ever imagine.

Kandace Davies:

God has brought situations and circumstances that have helped me understand the effort, time, tears, commitment, and steadfast love it takes to work out the ministry of reconciliation. God has allowed me to live out a reconciled life, and for that, I give Him the glory.

I echo Conrad's sentiments towards the many people in our lives who have been our cheerleaders before this work, during this work, and even those who will walk with us into the next work God has for us to do. Your support has been instrumental in reminding us that we have something to offer that others need in order to build up the Body of Christ.

ConRad-ical, you are the first person to truly teach me (and continue to teach me) what it means to be a team. As we have experienced in our marriage, being unified truly commands the blessing of God (Psalm 133:1-3)! I love you more and more each day! Thank you for being my best and trusted teammate in the Davies Clan!

TABLE OF CONTENTS

A Word of Prayer

Before you begin this process guide, we ask that you pray these scriptural prayers below. We highly recommend that you pray them out loud to the Lord:

> *Father, You are the author of life, and I trust the story You have told in the Bible (Genesis 1:1; 2:7; 2 Timothy 3:16-17).*
>
> *I ask that You reveal Your story about me and help me fulfill the purposes You created me for (Acts 13:36).*
>
> *I pray as King David prayed, "Search me, O God, and know my heart! Try me and know my thoughts! And see if there be any grievous way in me, and lead me in the way everlasting!" (Psalm 139:23-24).*
>
> *I confess that You are the Lord of my life (Romans 10:9).*
> *I lean not to my own understanding (Proverbs 3:5).*
> *I choose to acknowledge You in all of my ways (Proverbs 3:6).*
> *I trust Your direction and believe that Your Word is living and active (Hebrews 4:12).*
>
> *I trust that You are the author and the perfecter of my faith (Hebrews 12:2).*
>
> *As I proceed, give me a spirit of wisdom and revelation in the knowledge of You, and open the eyes of my heart in the name of Jesus (Ephesians 1:17-18)! Amen.*

Please don't skip over this prayer. We ask that you don't continue until you are prayerfully ready to go on this journey with us. Please remember the words of the Apostle Paul in Ephesians 6:12: "For we do not wrestle against flesh and blood, but against the rulers, against the authorities, against the cosmic powers over this present darkness, against the spiritual forces of evil in the heavenly places."

Any division in humanity results from sin (fortunately, Jesus fixed the sin problem at the cross). Furthermore, division usually starts with our adversary; thus, our weapons of choice are prayer and the Word of God.

This process guide is a journey and not a quick solution to all disunity issues. This journey is not easy, so we must remain prayerful.

Instructions

The Importance of Prayer

Prayer is the vehicle in which we receive and give communication to God. Recognizing that prayer is a two-way channel helps us see that there are times when we speak and times when we listen. God's standard of unity requires us to be willing to seek the face of the One who has the power to change our hearts. Prayer is a vulnerable and humble act, for when we pray, we acknowledge our need for One who is greater, stronger, and more powerful than we are.

We have included prayers at the end of each session to get you started, but don't stop there. Allow it to be a launching point into greater levels of repentance, petition, requests, and declarations to our Father in heaven. God has promised in His Word that He would heal our land by our seeking His face. So let's take Him at His Word and watch Him complete the work He has started in us as we seek His face in prayer. Never underestimate the power of prayer!

The Importance of Honesty

One of the most challenging things in our Western and American culture is to be fully honest without being self-deprecating or vitriolic. Honesty is the only way to access what is happening in our hearts and allow God's Word to transform us. Truth invites freedom into our souls. God's Word tells us that the heart is deceitful above all things (Jeremiah 17:9). When we honestly examine our hearts, we find hidden things that we do not want to admit. Fear, shame, hate, hurt—the list goes on of sin in our hearts. When God allows us to see what is there, don't ignore it. The more honest we are with ourselves and God, the more we will benefit from this Process Guide and the more healing we will experience.

Reading and Wrestling with the Scriptures

One of the most important spiritual disciplines for the believer to grow spiritually is reading the Bible. Reading devotionals and inspirational books is good, but the believer should learn how to draw conclusions from the Bible. We recommend reading a version such as the English Standard Version (ESV), the New American Standard Version (NASB), or even the New Living Translation (NLT). However, we recognize that people have their traditions and preferences; therefore, whatever version you read, make sure you read it regularly, prayerfully, thoughtfully, and voraciously; it is necessary and life-giving.

When we (Dr. Conrad & Kandace) read the Scriptures, we tend to read it systematically (e.g., yearly Bible reading plan or reading whole books at a time), for we strive to place the text and its verses in their proper cultural context. We don't want to read the Bible through the lens of our 21st century, Greco-Roman/British-influenced perspective, warping the author's original intention. We must keep in mind that the Bible is a Hebraic piece of literature birthed out of a Hebraic people who lived a Hebraic life and spoke a Hebraic language. The focus is that God wanted to set an example through one people group to educate the world on His nature.

Thus, the ultimate goal of studying is to understand the original cultural context (e.g., culture, language, author, historical events), make a proper interpretation, and apply the principles to your life. Studying is a daunting task, and it takes time. Therefore, we have avoided taking you on a technical study of learning language and cultural context for this Process Guide. Yet, we HIGHLY recommend you still put in the work to study (i.e., be like the Bereans in Acts 17:11).

Online Resources

We recommend some online sources to help you find, navigate, and study Scripture. Below is a list of a few online Bible resources, and each has some helpful links on their website to assist you.

Blue Letter Bible
https://www.blueletterBible.org/

According to Blue Letter Bible's website, they state that the Blue Letter Bible "provides powerful tools for an in-depth study of God's Word through our free online reference library, with study tools that are grounded in the historical, conservative Christian faith."

We recommend clicking on their HELP section to learn more about their website's navigation through video tutorials, helpful links, or contacting them. You can also do some introductory study of the original languages associated with the Bible through this Blue Letter Bible source.

Bible Hub
https://Biblehub.com/

"Bible Hub's mission is to 1) increase the visibility and accessibility of the Scriptures online, 2) provide free access to Bible study tools in many languages, and 3) promote the Gospel of Christ through the learning, study, and application of God's Word."

Our perspective is that this source is more technical, yet it is phenomenal regarding the user's depth when studying the original languages. This resource may be challenging to navigate, yet it gives more depth to one's study.

Bible Gateway
https://www.Biblegateway.com/

Bible Gateway is a "searchable online Bible in more than 200 versions and 70 languages that you can freely read, research, and reference anywhere. With a library of audio Bibles, a mobile app, devotionals, email newsletters, and other free resources, Bible Gateway equips you not only to *read* the Bible but to *understand* it."

We believe the Bible Gateway platform is the easiest to navigate and use when reading and searching for things throughout the Bible online. Yet, we don't see it as vital in studying the original languages like Blue Letter Bible and Bible Hub.

Use whatever resource to help you navigate the Bible best. We use all three of the above resources (both the websites and apps), and we navigate each one according to its purposes. Bible Gateway gives many versions of the Scriptures, quick reads, audio versions, and quick searches. Blue Letter Bible provides access to the original roots of words in the Scripture, and Bible Hub allows one to go deeper into the conjugations of words and trace different forms of the word throughout the Scriptures. Of course, we cross-reference each one all the time, yet that is just the way we choose to study the Scriptures.

You will find your patterns and create your resource lists if you don't have one. We just wanted to offer some free online resources to assist you on your journey.

Introduction

The devotional Process Guide you are reading will take you on a journey to a potentially new perspective of unity and reconciliation. You are someone whom God has called to be an agent of change in your respective sphere of influence, whether you are a stay-at-home mom, medical professional, educator, or college student. If you have said "Yes" to God and desire to know Him more, exercise your faith by walking on this journey towards unity.

Please note that the Gospel of the Lord Jesus Christ is the foundation of this journey. Thus, our message is for "Believers Only." Non-believers can participate, but they must keep in mind that no other philosophy on the planet facilitates people to unite like the Gospel. Thus, Fellow Believers, you are encouraged to remember who you are in Christ, remember your calling in Christ, and remember God's mandate for you as His child. We need to minimize and leave the opinions of popular culture and proceed to communicate according to the expectations of God's kingdom. We must live and speak according to God's ways in all contexts for us to see fundamental changes. Therefore, in partnership with the Holy Spirit, allow us to walk with you as fellow travelers and brethren. We will mutually encourage one another on the journey since we need you and you need us (Ephesians 4).

Overview of the Process Guide

We have outlined the Process Guide below. There will be seven conversations around different topics to prepare us to engage one another and the world. In Session 1, we will examine "The Power of Language." Sessions 2—6 will go through a five-part journey towards unity as outlined in Ephesians 4:1-6. The five-part process explores History, Humility, Hurt, Hunger, and Harmony. Finally, in Session 7, we will consider our calling and appropriate action steps based on what God is putting on our hearts to do. We trust that the Holy Spirit will give you specific action steps along the way and at the journey's end.

Process Guide Sessions:

	Title	The Focus
1	The Conversation about the Power of Language	Worldview
2	The Conversation about History	The Context of Disunity
3	The Conversation about Humility	Character
4	The Conversation about Hurt	Experiences
5	The Conversation about Hunger	Desires
6	The Conversation about Harmony	Goals
7	The Conversation about YOU Being Called!	Action Steps

Staying at the Table

We recognize that there are two separate contexts for having conversations about unity and reconciliation. One context is at the "dinner table" amongst believers. The other context is with those who are under the world's system of beliefs. Believers already have unity in the Spirit because of the work of Jesus Christ on the cross. Believers hash out unity with others who know our King and know His heart at the table. We learn not to get up from the table and learn how to have hard conversations. The other context for our discussions is with the world (i.e., the society); it seeks the unity and reconciliation that God has already provided yet uses methods that are philosophically different from God's Hebraic way. Thus, Believers in Jesus need to be trained in God's ways at the dinner table and then influence the world's system on how God does unity. Simply, we must learn the Kingdom way by staying at the dinner table and then disciple the world to follow God's way.

Reading Focus

Last, we would like you to read the letter by the Apostle Paul to the Ephesians before, during, and after you start the sessions. The letter is six chapters long, and it is all about unity.

We are so excited about your journey!

As we move forward in our conversations, remember to walk in God's P.O.W.E.R:

Pray without ceasing.

Open your heart to what He has to say.

Wrestle with the Scriptures.

Eat His Words daily, for they are food for you.

Reflect on and remember His promises!

SESSION 1: The Conversation about the Power of Language

SCRIPTURAL THOUGHT:

> *"So He (Jesus) said to the Jews who had believed Him, "If you continue in My Word, you are truly My disciples. Then you will know the truth, and the truth will set you free."* (John 8:31-32, ESV)

READING FOR THE DAY:

> *John 17 (Jesus' High Priestly prayer)*

FORMATION OF CULTURE

Distinct cultures and nations have formed because of the language division resulting from man's rebellion at the Tower of Babel (Genesis 11). This confusion of language resulted in groups of people settling in different parts of the world, establishing various ways of living, other languages, different traditions, and, over time, creating distinct physical characteristics.

God created humanity in His image (Genesis 1:26-27), and He placed all the necessary information in the human DNA to make various skin tones, hair textures, and facial features. Even with the variety of diverse physical characteristics, we are all still of one essence: human. The nature of how melanin functions in our humanity is no different, for we are just different shades of brown. Thus, the types of division(s) we see amongst nations and peoples today (e.g., racism, denominations) are not a part of God's original design but a human socio-cultural construction.

For the sake of example, let's explore the hot topic of the term "race." It will help us demonstrate how language affects our worldview, and we will gain a biblical understanding of "race" and evaluate it against God's original intentions for humanity.

DECONSTRUCTING "RACE"

Race is a word passed down for generations after the Enlightenment period. We've heard it spoken by the media, teachers, parents, and even in the pulpit of our churches. Most of us wouldn't critically think about the word *race* and its use in our world today. Educational systems teach about Charles Darwin and how he divided people groups into "distinct races," or we may have learned about Immanuel Kant, John Locke, or Louis Agassiz's work. Yet, we may not have thought critically about their work.

Have you ever thought about the concept of "race" in the Bible?

Here are two English online dictionary definitions:

Merriam-Webster Dictionary Online:
1) any one of the groups that humans are often divided into based on physical traits regarded as common among people of shared ancestry
2) *also:* the fact of dividing people, or of people being divided, into such groups: categorization by race
3) *dated:* a group of people sharing a common cultural, geographical, linguistic, or religious origin or background
4) *archaic:* the descendants of a common ancestor: a group sharing a common lineage

American Heritage Dictionary Online:
1) A group of people identified as distinct from other groups because of supposed physical or genetic traits shared by the group. Most biologists and anthropologists do not recognize race as a biologically valid classification, in part because there is more genetic variation within groups than between them.
2) A group of people united or classified together on the basis of common history, nationality, or geographic distribution: the Celtic race.
3) A genealogical line; a lineage
4) Humans considered as a group

PROCESS QUESTIONS ABOUT RACE

1. Using an online Bible search tool (see the Instructions section of this guide for some options), search for the word *race* and read the Scriptures in your search results (mainly use newer translations like the NIV, ESV, NASB, and others). What themes do you notice about "race" in these Scriptures?

_____

_____

_____

_____

2. How do the online dictionary definitions compare to how it is used in the Scripture?

_____

_____

_____

_____

3. Do another online Bible search tool for the word *race,* yet focus specifically on the older Bible versions (e.g., Geneva, KJV, Wycliffe). What are some of the differences between the results of the newer translations (e.g., NIV, NASB, ESV) and the older translations?

_____

_____

_____

_____

English translators created the Geneva Bible and the King James Version (KJV) before the influence of the Enlightenment period on the world's cultures. Thus, *race* was not integrated into the vernacular of the English translations of the Bible before this time. Yet, many translations after the Enlightenment period combined race as a part of their translations to help us understand people groups better. Unfortunately, the newer translations have perpetuated the dehumanization of humanity by using the term.

The reality is that the modern understanding of "race" is a social construct, not a biblical truth established by God. Charles Darwin, an evolutionary biologist, and his prior and current contemporaries developed and used the term *race* to dehumanize humanity by categorizing humans like animals. Dangerously, they classified certain "races" of people as having higher capacity, higher reasoning, higher intellectual thought, and higher survivability than other "races" of humans. All humans are of higher order, have more complexity, and have a higher capacity for reasoning than animals, and all humans are created equally in God's image. Humans should not be categorized or viewed like animals and plants. In simple terms, anytime we use the word *race,* we dehumanize the beauty of God's diversity and complexity.

For further study, review Darwin's 1859 published work titled: On the Origin of Species by Means of Natural Selection, on the Preservation of Favoured Races in the Struggle for Life. *Also, consider the title of Darwin's famous work. Does it sound socio-cultural or biblical?*

The *closest* word that corresponds with the concept of "race" is the word *kind,* as identified in the creation story in the book of Genesis.

4. Do a search on the word *kind* in the Scriptures, especially in the book of Genesis. What do these scriptures refer to—plants/animals or humans? (See Genesis 1:25 and 2:9.)

_____

_____

_____

_____

5. Why do you think there has been such an emphasis on the term *race* in American society?

_____

_____

_____

_____

6. Read Acts 17:26-31. These verses refer to us all being from "one man." How does the concept of "race" challenge this biblical truth?

_____

_____

_____

_____

PRAYER FOR SESSION ONE:

Show me Your ways, Lord; teach me Your ways that lead to Your truth, and when I see Your truth, guide me in Your truth and teach me, for You are my God, my Savior. May I not lean on my own understanding but acknowledge You in all my ways and allow You to direct my paths. Thank You that You are the Way, the Truth, and the Life. Help me not just to know the truth but do it so that You may make me free. I receive all that You have for me today. In Jesus' name, I pray, Amen. (Prayers from Psalm 25:4-5; Proverbs 3:5-6; Psalm 145:18; John 14:6; 8:31-32)

BE RECONCILED

SESSION 2: The Conversation about History

SCRIPTURAL THOUGHT:

"I, therefore, a prisoner of the Lord, urge you to walk in a manner worthy of the calling for which you have been called..." (Ephesians 4:1, ESV)

READING FOR THE DAY:

Ephesians 1

HISTORY: WHAT IS THE CONTEXT OF THE JOURNEY?

If one were to view me (Dr. Conrad) based on the concept of "race," a person would get an incorrect assumption of my life. First of all, I am a 6-foot-tall, athletic-build, darker brown-skinned man who wears glasses. Because of my name, Conrad Alfred Patrick Davies, some have assumed that I am an older, fair-skinned, European male with wealth, yet one may not know the rich and deep cultural context from which I've come. Sadly, my skin color has connoted specific culturally-trained characteristics about who I am. Consider Session 1 and see how the socio-cultural term *race* gets more confusing when applied to my story.

Please view a picture of my family and me in the About Us section of the Process Guide.

I (Dr. Conrad) start us on the journey towards unity by intentionally telling my story to lay a foundation for our direction. Remember that every journey of unity, whether in a marriage, in a friendship, or between cultures, has a context. We must always consider where someone has come from before we move forward. The goal is to gain sympathy, empathy, and compassion.

My parents were born and raised as Krio people in the small West African country of Sierra Leone. Krios are ex-American and British slaves who returned to the African continent, and the British colonists "rehabilitated" them in Britain's crown colony called the Sierra Leone Colony.

My parents immigrated to the United States in the 1970s. They birthed three children: my sister, my brother, and me. Combined, my parents have seven university degrees (three bachelor's degrees and four master's degrees). Their three children have eight degrees combined (three bachelor's, three master's, and two doctorates). All three children were lettered Division One college athletes while managing rigorous undergraduate chemistry degree programs (i.e., all three children have at least one chemistry degree).

Our family had a multi-ethnic experience in the US. We lived and engaged primarily in the central Kentucky version of African communities, white-American communities, black-American communities, and several other ethnic communities (e.g., various Spanish-speaking people groups, Bosnians, Indians). We befriended, intimately loved, and trusted people from all over the world.

Yet, each family member has also experienced prejudice and discrimination based on their unique experiences living in Kentucky. My parents' perspective was as educated foreign immigrants wanting a better opportunity. The children's perspective was as highly educated, first-generation American-born black kids with a diverse cultural perspective who never felt like we fit in.

God has redeemed and used our story in His Kingdom. Our context has helped us to transcend cultural boundaries and connect with people of different ethnicities. For instance, my younger brother, who has a Ph.D. in Biochemistry, is a chemist in California who leads a diverse yet predominantly Asian-descent Bible study group in his home. I am a university educator who has mentored, counseled, and loved all sorts of students (e.g., varieties of Americans and international students from all over the world). My sister engages and leads many different people in her professional context as a Project Manager in California. We each have had experiences of individuals simply taking their prejudices and poorly classifying us by their racially-trained standards. They have missed opportunities to connect with our hearts because "race" constructs perpetuated disunity in certain relationships.

Unfortunately, dehumanizing racial classifications such as "Black" American, rather than Sierra Leonean-American or Krio of Sierra Leone, have had people miss the fullness of our cultural identity. Some people have missed our context, which has formed elements of our identity.

Let's turn our attention to the Bible for some more insights.

PROCESS QUESTIONS ABOUT HISTORY:
PETER AND CORNELIUS

The Apostle Peter has just experienced a lame man healed and a woman raised from the dead in his ministry (Acts 9), and he is now staying at the house of a man named Simon, a tanner. Chapter 10 picks up by discussing powerful encounters with God by both Peter and Cornelius. They are culturally different from one another, but eventually, God unifies them for the sake of the Gospel.

Read the book of Acts 10:1 through 11:18.

1. What is Cornelius's cultural context? What is his role and his position? (Acts 10:1-2, 22)

_____

_____

_____

_____

2. What is Peter's cultural context? What is his background? (Acts 10:14, 28)

_____

_____

_____

_____

For generations, the Jewish people considered all Gentiles inherently unclean. To gain some brief insights on uncleanness, do an online Bible search on the word *unclean* and read the scriptures. The Levitical law, other Scriptures, along with commentary from religious leaders, would have helped create the context for Peter's worldview.

3. What is the disunity between these two men?

_____

_____

_____

_____

4. Consider Peter's statement in Acts 10:28. What changed in Peter?

_____

_____

_____

_____

5. In your life, consider your cultural context. What value do you bring to the Kingdom of God because of your cultural perspective?

_____

_____

_____

_____

6. Consider how God has spoken to you about your identity.

_____

_____

_____

_____

7. Consider how God has navigated your life through different experiences.

_____

_____

_____

_____

8. How did Peter and Cornelius become unified? (Acts 10:4-6, 15, 28, 31-32, 34-43, 10:44-48)

_____

_____

_____

_____

9. How did Peter's friends respond when Peter and the other circumcised believers returned to report what happened? (Acts 11:2-3)

_____

_____

_____

_____

10. If you embraced people of various cultural backgrounds, how do you think people in your circles would respond to you? Consider the previous question.

_____

_____

_____

_____

11. Based on the story, what are some of the perceived requirements that one needs to consider to go on a journey towards unity like Peter and Cornelius? (Acts 10:3-6, 9-17, 29-34, 44; 11:4)

_____

_____

_____

_____

12. Like Peter, is there anything you would need to turn from to help your journey towards unity based on your cultural traditions?

_____

_____

_____

_____

13. The context of all disunity comes from sin. What can we learn from how God brought about reconciliation between Himself and humanity (Romans 5:6-11; 2 Corinthians 5:18-21; Colossians 1:15-23)? How has this affected you?

_____

_____

_____

_____

PRAYER FOR SESSION TWO:

Lord, as You called Peter to affect Cornelius's whole household, help me walk in a manner worthy of the calling for which I have been called (Ephesians 4:1; Colossians 1:10). Speak to my heart as You spoke to Peter's. In my times of prayer with You, will You affect my heart where I ponder my cultural upbringing, and You prepare me for action (1 Peter 3:15)? Show me any prejudiced thinking and give me the grace to repent and renounce sin as You reveal it to me. Show me the truth. I want to be free to worship You and be an ambassador of reconciliation in this world. In Jesus' name, I ask these things. Amen.

SESSION 3: The Conversation about Humility

SCRIPTURAL THOUGHT:

> *"...with all humility, gentleness, and patience..."* (Ephesians 4:2, ESV)

READING FOR THE DAY:

> *Ephesians 2*

THE HEART OF HUMILITY

God is the chief reconciler, and this dense yet straightforward phrase packages the story of unity: *The Offended Restores the Offender.*

Consider the Gospel story. "God became a man in Jesus the Christ. Jesus lived the life we should have lived and died the death we should have died in our place. Three days later, He rose from the dead, proving that He is the Son of God and offering the gift of salvation and the forgiveness of sins to anyone who repents and believes in Him" *(created by Ps. Rice Broocks, co-founder of Every Nation Ministries).*

Let's rephrase the story:

God created all things in, and through, and for Himself, *is offended* by His representatives on earth (i.e., humans) who choose to rebel against Him by their disobedience to His command (Genesis 1—3). From the beginning, God chooses to pursue, cover, and redeem the effects of humanity's disobedience, by becoming like humanity in Jesus (i.e., the second Adam) to fix the sin problem in the relationship. The offenders (i.e., all of humanity) now can receive the gift of salvation and pardon for their wrongdoing because God did the work through Jesus to restore the Offended and the offender's relationship. Thus, God, the Offended, relationally restores the offenders, humanity.

Ponder this in the context of most human relationships:

What if the offended party offered forgiveness to the offender?

What if the offended party imitated God's pattern of unity?

What if the offended party loved their offender the way God loved His offenders, humanity?

We must remember that forgiveness is a spiritual, grace-filled matter by which the Holy Spirit must empower a person to do the things that God did through Jesus. The offended party must be empowered to forgive, which does not justify what the offender did as right. Still, it keeps the relationship open by minimizing bitterness, hatred, and "cancer" to the soul.

These principles specifically focus on cultural, theological, ideological, emotional, and spiritual areas of disunity. Forgiveness is necessary for personal healing, but one must put boundaries in place in physically or emotionally dangerous situations. We cannot expect every relationship to be restored to a healthy union since both the offended and the offender must work together to seek healing from our heavenly Father and have peace in their soul (Romans 12:18).

As we consider the character trait of humility, consider how God had to humble himself. As the offended party, God took a critical step to humble Himself to satisfy the journey towards unity, not just the offending party. Too often, we perceive that offenders should only humble themselves and ask for forgiveness. However, the offended party must humble themselves to fully satisfy the unity journey so that the relationship can be potentially restored. Paul, in Ephesians 4:2, tells us to go on the journey with "ALL humility, gentleness, and patience." Ponder this.

Let's turn our attention to more scriptures to process the following questions.

PROCESS QUESTIONS ABOUT HUMILITY

Read Philippians 2:1-11.

1. As you read the passage, what stood out to you in the scripture?

_____

_____

_____

_____

2. What do you learn about humanity in this scripture?

_____

_____

_____

_____

3. What do you learn about God in this scripture?

_____

_____

_____

_____

4. What applies to you, and how is it applicable to some circumstance(s) of disunity in your life?

_____

_____

_____

_____

5. Consider the offending party in your circumstance. How could that person apply verses 3 and 4?

_____

_____

_____

_____

6. Consider who is the offended party in your circumstance. How could that person apply verses 3 and 4?

_____

_____

_____

_____

7. Why is it essential for the offended party to humble themselves?

_____

_____

_____

_____

8. Connect the verses above with Colossians 3:5-14. What is similar? What is different? What is challenging for you?

_____

_____

_____

_____

9. Connect Jesus' words in the Gospel of John 10:14-18 to other scriptures read today. How does the Good Shepherd show humility?

_____

_____

_____

_____

10. What is the Spirit of God convicting you to do based on what you
    have read in His Word? How are you going to respond?

_____

_____

_____

_____

More Scriptures for Reflection:

Proverbs 11:2
Proverbs 15:33
Proverbs 18:12
Proverbs 22:4

PRAYER FOR SESSION THREE:

*Lord, as one who has greatly offended You through my rebellion,
disobedience, and sin, You have shown me great compassion by for-
giving me and restoring me to a relationship with You. So, whether
I'm the offender or the offended, help me humble myself before
You and those of which I am disunified. I ask for Your grace to
allow me to forgive others. I ask for Your grace to be gentle and
patient with those who have offended me. Open my heart to value
others above myself and look to the interests of others. Help me to
be patient and gentle with those I have offended. I need Your help.
Amen.*

SESSION 4: The Conversation about Hurt

SCRIPTURAL THOUGHT:

"...bearing with one another in love..." (Ephesians 4:2, ESV)

READING FOR THE DAY:

Ephesians 3

THE REALITY OF HURT

The depravity of the human heart has left us all broken. We have all been wounded and have wounded others (i.e., Hurt people hurt people). We experienced our first hurts through the ones we knew the most within our family of origin. Psalm 51:5 says, "We are shaped in iniquity and sin at our mother's womb." The Hebrew word *shaped* means to "twist" in iniquity (i.e., perversion, depravity, wrong thinking). Due to sin, there is a way that we have been formed or "shaped" that affects the way we relate to those around us, especially to those who are closest to us.

Our emotional and intellectual responses to opposition, opinions, and actions different from ours started forming as early as our first challenging encounter. As physical wounds are tender to the touch, so are our emotional wounds that come from our souls. Also, like physical wounds, the quicker we tend to them, the faster they can undergo the healing process. But the hard part is to "allow" ourselves to go through the process of hurt in a way that allows us to heal properly. Letting ourselves go through the process is the biggest stumbling block of experiencing hurt. Experiencing pain is inevitable, and if we want reconciliation (2 Corinthians 5:18), we should expect that hurt and pain are part of the human experience. However, God has given us what we need to process hurt, and we can experience healing and reconciliation on the other side. Let us please not rush to the other side; we need to heal correctly.

PROCESS QUESTIONS ABOUT HURT

1. As a child, who would be the first person (people) you would run to when you were hurt emotionally or physically?

   _____

   _____

   _____

   _____

2. What was their typical response to your hurt?

   _____

   _____

   _____

   _____

3. Is this a typical response you get from others now when you experience hurt?

   _____

   _____

   _____

   _____

4. Think of another time someone hurt you emotionally. Were you able to process through the hurt, or did you have another response to the healing process (e.g., stuffed it away, ignored it, stonewalled)? Explain your answer.

   _____

   _____

   _____

   _____

SIX STEPS TO PROCESS THROUGH HURT

Steps	Scriptural References
Acknowledge that you are hurting	Psalm 55:22
Identify why it hurts	Proverbs 4:7; 20:5
Face the reality of why it hurts (i.e., acceptance)	Proverbs 28:13; James 4:1-4
Welcome the Holy Spirit in the place of hurt	Psalms 5:31; 34:18; 71:20; 147:3; Isa. 41:10; Matt. 11:28

Steps	Scriptural References
Allow yourself time to process and heal	Psalm 30:5; Ecclesiastes 3:3b
Make the necessary steps to walk in peace again (e.g., with yourself, the person, the situation, the circumstance).	Isaiah 43:18; John 14:27; Romans 12:18; Colossians 3:12-14

(*More of this process will be developed in our future book,* Be Reconciled: A Journey Towards Unity)

5. Which of the six steps above are the most challenging for you to do when you experience hurt in a relationship? Why do you think so? (This does not necessarily include physical or sexual hurt.)

_____

_____

_____

_____

6. What barriers hinder you from not taking steps to walk in peace with the person again?

_____

_____

_____

_____

Peace does not necessarily mean you are best friends with the offender or have to create a level of closeness/intimacy with this person. Your experiencing peace also does not mean the other person has to be at peace with you. They are responsible for the decisions they make and in their relationship with God. The focus is you and your ability to find wholeness (e.g., unbroken emotions, fellowship) with God regardless of anyone else's actions.

7. Pray and ask God if there are any current hurt(s) in your heart due to a relationship in your life (e.g., spouse, children, extended family, friends, work relationships, acquaintances). Write their names down below.

_____

_____

_____

_____

Review the six steps again and apply them. We trust that God can and will help you heal and be whole in your relationships.

More Scriptures for Reflection:

Matthew 6:14-15
1 John 1:8-9

PRAYER FOR SESSION FOUR:

Father, I do not like to be hurt. Yet You knew that we would all experience pain within the human experience because of sin. Thank You for making provision for the hurts in my life by coming to heal and bind up my wounds when I am brokenhearted (Psalm 147:3). Help me to trust the process that You have made available for me. I receive the peace that You left me, and I will not let fear of this process overtake me (John 14:27). I ask this of You in Jesus' name, Amen.

SESSION 5: The Conversation about Hunger

SCRIPTURAL THOUGHT:

"...eager to maintain the unity of the Spirit in the bond of peace."
(Ephesians 4:3, ESV)

READING FOR THE DAY:

Ephesians 4

ARE YOU HUNGRY?

Session 4 identified the hurt and healing process necessary for the journey towards unity. Yet, once healing has started, we must be eager to maintain a desire to build relationships again. We must choose to resume our prior relational activities and not lose hope in what possibil-ities exist. For instance, consider the human body. One sign of sickness in the body is a loss of appetite. A person begins to not desire food, and the manifestation of the illness begins to show itself. A loss of appetite will continue until the sickness subsides and the desire to eat returns. The same can sometimes be true with experiencing hurt and healing from that hurt. We can lose our desire to want to unify with another.

Do you hunger for unity with your brethren?
If we recognize that we are not hungry for unity and reconciliation, we can ask God to make us hungry. We can acknowledge apathy and passivity to God and repent for ways we have not been eager to maintain the unity of the Spirit in the bond of peace. When we seek God, we will find Him. When we ask, we will receive from Him.

In the next section, consider the diversity of God's kingdom, for the Body of Christ is diverse and complex like the human body. As you pro-cess, think where you fit in His kingdom and if you are willing to remain hungry for unity with your brethren, especially those different from you. God has beautifully created unity in diversity.

PROCESS QUESTIONS FOR HUNGER

Read Romans 12:3-8 (be sure to read context).

1. What are the *grace gifts*?

_____

_____

_____

Read 1 Corinthians 12:4-11 (be sure to read context).

2. What are the *manifestations of the Spirit* for the common good?

_____

_____

_____

Read Ephesians 4:11-16 and 1 Corinthians 12:27-31 (be sure to read context).

3. Who did God give to the Body of Christ to build her up? Who did God appoint?

_____

_____

_____

Pause for a moment and look back at the three different lists.

Read the context (preferably the whole chapter) of what the Apostle Paul says to these three different churches if you haven't already.

4. What seems to be some themes across the three different chapters? Why do you think the Apostle Paul identified these gifts, manifestations, and roles?

_____

_____

_____

Did you notice the diversity of the Body?

The diversity of gifts, manifestations, and roles challenges unity in the Body of Christ. Therefore, God has called us to bear with one another (Ephesians 4:2; Colossians 3:13), be in unity with one another (Psalm 133:1, Ephesians 4:1, 3, 13; 1 Peter 3:8), and love one another (John 13:34-35; 15:12, 17; Hebrews 10:24; 1 John 4:7). Unity with our brethren is not about being the same (i.e., functioning in the same roles, having the same gifts, or experiencing the same manifestations); it is about submission to the function of where God has placed us in the Body of Christ for His glory and honoring our brethren's position in the Body. In other words, unity requires a willingness to mutually submit to our brethren and submit to God (Ephesians 5:17-21).

God loves all types of diversity within the things He created, yet He does not like "ideological" diversity. In other words, He desires complete submission to *His ways* and *His authority,* yet diversity in systems contrary to His, or listening to voices other than His, makes God angry. He desires sole allegiance to His voice, His systems, His ways, and His jurisdiction: Lordship.

5. Write about some of your challenges with staying eager to maintain unity in a relationship with your brethren. What happened to cause the disunity? Allow these thoughts to prepare you for Session 6.

_____

_____

_____

_____

More Scriptures for Reflection:

Proverbs 4:7
Matthew 5:23-24
Matthew 18:15
Romans 12:9-18
Romans 14—15
Ephesians 3:15-21
Ephesians 4:31-32
Hebrews 13:17

PRAYER FOR SESSION FIVE:

Father, help me to stand up for the truth even when I am afraid. Give me the courage to ask You for growth in hunger towards maintaining the unity of peace with my brethren. Increase my desire for unity among those around me. Let me be quick to lay down any gifts to You on the altar for me to be reconciled to my brethren. Increase my hunger for unity. In Jesus' name, Amen.

SESSION 6: The Conversation about Harmony

SCRIPTURAL THOUGHT:

"There is one body and one Spirit—just as you were called to the one hope that belongs to your call—one Lord, one faith, one baptism, one God and Father of all, who is over all and through all and in all..." (Ephesians 4:4-6, ESV)

READING FOR THE DAY:

Ephesians 5

THE ONE CONDUCTOR: GOD

In the last session, we thought about challenges in staying eager to maintain unity with our brethren. Let us now use a word picture of an orchestra and its conductor to summarize this whole journey towards unity. One conductor leads a diversity of instrumentalists towards a common goal of finding harmony in a piece of music.

The conductor keeps the tempo of every part of the song and keeps the musicians together and on track. The conductor must know the music (e.g., loudness or softness, tempo) and when to start and stop the orchestra accordingly. The conductor may be coordinating hundreds of people, and everyone's eyes should always be on the conductor.

Everything the conductor does should convey a cohesive musical message.

For the instrumentalists, the focus is to know their instrument and look and submit to the conductor.

For our purposes, God is the Conductor of many ethnic expressions of His ways. He alone can lead such levels of diversity, and He alone knows the tempo and the sound of the music He wants to communicate to the world. He alone can handle the magnificence of the work on the earth that tells the world He came to save us (John 17:20-23).

The process questions below use Ananias and Paul's story in Acts 9 to help us analyze how the two men eventually walked in harmony.

PROCESS QUESTIONS ABOUT HARMONY

Read Acts 9:1-19. Answer the following questions using the above metaphorical imagery of an orchestra.

1. Who is the conductor? Who are the instruments in this story?

_____

_____

_____

_____

2. What are some ways that may have hindered Paul and Ananias's ability to submit to the Conductor? (Acts 9:1-2, 13-14)

_____

_____

_____

_____

3. What is the Lord's (i.e., the Conductor's) reason for instructing Ananias to meet with Paul? (Acts 9:15-16)

_____

_____

_____

_____

4. What are some of the results of God putting Ananias and Paul together?

_____

_____

_____

_____

5. What glorifies God in putting these two men together?

_____

_____

_____

_____

6. Observe the bigger story God is telling. Consider how He connected Ananias and Paul, specifically in Damascus. Share your thoughts on how you see God's hand in the bigger story. (Acts 9:3, 6, 8, 10-11, 17)

_____

_____

God used the offended party (Ananias) to restore the offender (Paul) all under the banner of Christ.

7. From what you know or have read from the Scriptures, would these two men have come together if God had not spoken to them? Why or why not?

_____

_____

_____

_____

8. Referring back to the orchestra analogy, although there are many different instruments, explain why when varieties of instruments play together, they make a beautiful sound.

_____

_____

_____

_____

9. What reason(s) would make the sound not be musical or harmonious? Apply the metaphor to your life (or to other relationships).

_____

_____

_____

_____

More Scriptures for Reflection:

Luke 17:3-4
John 17
Romans 5:10-11
1 Corinthians 1:10
2 Corinthians 5:19

PRAYER FOR SESSION SIX:

Father, I put aside my preconceived ideas of the people around me based on their background. I will respond to Your leading to love and serve my brethren that may seem different than me. Help me to stay focused on You as the Conductor (Lord) of my life. Please forgive me for questioning the way You choose to handle Your chosen instruments. Amen.

RECONCILED

SESSION 7: The Conversation about YOU Being Called!

SCRIPTURAL THOUGHT:

"But grace was given to each one of us according to the measure of Christ's gift." (Ephesians 4:7, ESV)

READING FOR THE DAY:

Ephesians 6

STIRRING THE GIFT AND CALL

If you are a child of God (John 1:12), you have a part to play in displaying the grace God has given you. No one who belongs to Christ is left out. We have all been called to walk in whatever gift (Ephesians 4:11) He has given us to build up the Body of Christ (Ephesians 4:12). We need all of us working together to equip and encourage one another so that the Body of Christ will be mature (Ephesians 4:13).

Consider just a few examples of the Apostle Paul's words about his and others' calling:

Scriptural Examples of Calling	Scripture
"...called to be an apostle"	Romans 1:1
"...including you who are called to belong to Jesus Christ"	Romans 1:6
"...who are loved by God and called to be saints"	Romans 1:7
"...for those who are called according to his purpose"	Romans 8:28
"And those whom he predestined, he also called, and those whom he called he also justified"	Romans 8:30
"For the gifts and the calling of God are irrevocable."	Romans 11:29
"Paul, called by the will of God to be an apostle of Christ Jesus..."	1 Corinthians 1:1

Scriptural Examples of Calling	Scripture
"...called to be saints together with all those who in every place call upon the name of our Lord Jesus Christ, both their Lord and ours"	1 Corinthians 1:2
"God is faithful, by whom you were called into the fellowship of his Son, Jesus Christ our Lord."	1 Corinthians 1:9
"...but to those who are called, both Jews and Greeks, Christ the power of God and the wisdom of God.	1 Corinthians 1:24

God gave us the grace to accomplish His purposes on the earth. Each of us has a uniqueness to our calling. We need you, and you need us, and we need to do this together, yet we need to continue on the journey of unity to do it all together.

SIMPLIFYING THE JOURNEY TOWARDS UNITY

Below is a simplified chart of a journey towards unity so that you have a quick reference. In this final session, let the Holy Spirit reveal what's happening in your heart so that you can experience the fullness of what God has for you. We are all called by God to fulfill a purpose, and we cannot allow disunity to hold us back.

The Phase of the Journey	Our Role on the Journey
History	We need to understand and recognize the disunity in the relationship. This phase is about gaining compassion, sympathy, and empathy.
Humility	We need to proceed forward with a posture of humility, gentleness, and patience. This phase is about character development.
Hurt	We must process the hurt(s) we feel in the relationship. This phase is about dealing with the pain and discomfort we will encounter.
Hunger	We must remain healthy by keeping up our appetite (i.e., desire) for unity. This phase is about remaining disciplined to maintain the unity of the Spirit.
Harmony	We must all submit and keep our eyes focused on the Conductor. This phase is about the goal of our journey: Oneness.

PROCESS QUESTIONS ABOUT YOUR CALLING

1. What are some areas of your life where you are living in disunity with God or your brethren?

_____

_____

_____

_____

2. Which phase of the journey seems most challenging for you?

_____

_____

_____

_____

3. What do you think God is calling you to do?

_____

_____

_____

_____

4. What do you think God is saying to you specifically?

_____

_____

_____

_____

5. What step can you take today to respond to what God is saying or calling you to do?

_____

_____

_____

_____

PRAYER FOR SESSION SEVEN:

Father, I recognize that You have called me to participate in Your divine nature. Will You open the eyes of my heart to respond to what You would have me to do? Help me see my brethren as You see them, and help me love them as You love them. When Your people are as one, You say that it tells the world that You were sent (John 17:20-23). I recognize that our unity is evangelism to the world, and it commands Your blessing. I want the world to know You. Amen.

OUR BLESSING AND PRAYER FOR YOU

Since we have now experienced the journey towards unity, we hope you have gained a framework you can use whenever there is disunity. We hope you have caught some revelations that we have learned that unity is not a quick process to obtain; it is a long journey. Reconsider how long God's journey for unity took in the Scriptures.

Our goal was not to provide a quick solution but to help show how God has created a narrow road for unity that must be maintained. He already did the heavy work of establishing unity, yet we have the ministry of reconciliation to maintain unity in the bond of peace. Each can choose to go on the journey, but it can be long, arduous, and challenging.

Therefore, if you desire more from us about this topic, please feel free to reach out, and we can help your ministries, marriages, workgroups, or work teams reach and accomplish their goals. Remember, this is always a journey, not a simple fix.

Let us pray for you:

> *"Lord, bless and keep our Friends. Turn Your face towards them and be gracious to them. Lift Your countenance towards them and grant them Your peace (Numbers 6:24). May the peace that surpasses all of their understanding guard their heart and mind in You (Philippians 4). Lord, we ask that You help them grasp the width, length, height, and depth of Your love that surpasses their knowledge (Ephesians 3). Give them the supernatural ability to see what You see, feel what You feel, love as You love, for Your perspective is most important in everything we do.*

> *Lord, we love them, and we bless them. In Jesus' name, Amen."*

WHAT'S NEXT?

Finally, this work is just the beginning. Our half-day, full-day, or conference-style workshops help you walk through each of these sessions. Our book provides more in-depth insights, and our video sessions offer commentary and other information to help you.

We ask that you don't simply end here but consider some of the other materials that will be available on our BE Reconciled website: http://www.bereconciledlexington.com.

FEEDBACK, QUESTIONS, & CONTACT INFORMATION

Please contact us with any feedback and/or questions:

Davies & Associates, LLC:
info@daviesassociatesllc.com
http://www.daviesassociatesllc.com

Dr. Conrad Davies:
conrad@daviesassociatesllc.com

Kandace Davies:
kandace@daviesassociatesllc.com

ABOUT US

The Davies' are catalysts of change to bring ethnic unity to Lexington, KY, and their mission is "The Offended Party Restores the Offender." The Davies' are a reconciled family who has helped lay the groundwork of an Every Nation Ministries (www.everynationlexington.org) church plant in Lexington, Kentucky.

The Davies teach people how to seek God through prayer, grow in leadership, live as marketplace ministers, grow in marriage, build family, and help people live in unity and reconciliation within the kingdom of God.

As bi-vocational missionaries, Dr. Conrad and Kandace Davies help lead a University of Kentucky campus ministry called Every Nation Campus (ENC). Dr. Conrad is a full-time Faculty Lecturer at the University of Kentucky, a training and development consultant, and a member of the board of Word Made Flesh, International. Kandace is a homemaker, friend, mother, and intercessor. She formerly had leadership roles with Mothers of Preschoolers International (MOPS) and Bible Study Fellowship International (BSF). She was on the board of a local nonprofit organization called Equipping Lydia.

The Davies started an organization called Davies & Associates, LLC (www.daviesassociatesllc.com), where they A.ctivate, C.ultivate, and E.mpower (A.C.E.) people to reach their full potential. Dr. Conrad is a Gallup-certified strength development coach and offers strengths-based workshops and training, individual strengths coaching, and executive coaching. Kandace and Dr. Conrad conduct specialized ministry workshops on intercession, prayer, unity, and reconciliation for the Body of Christ. They want everyone to be an A.C.E. in all that they do.

The Davies family of five includes three world-changing children: Conrad, Jr. (CJ), Levi, and Sarah Arden.

We thank you for your support in what Jesus is doing in Lexington, Kentucky, and its surrounding areas.

Made in the USA
Middletown, DE
17 January 2022

58461359R00027